# Investing In Gold and Silver While Managing Debt

Roggie Clark

## Avoid Credit Card Debt With This Book

Are you tired of living paycheck to paycheck? Drowning in interest rates and minimum payments that never seem to shrink your balance? *Understanding & Overcoming Credit Card Debt* is your roadmap to financial freedom.

https://www.amazon.com/dp/B0F3WCVWG8

## Avoid Wasting Money On Crypto With This Book

Whether you're curious, cautious, or ready to invest, this book breaks down complex topics into plain language and cuts through the noise, buzzwords, and get-rich-quick schemes.

https://www.amazon.com/Think-Before-You-Crypto-Understanding-ebook/dp/B0F3YQ1L2Q

## Learn How To Invest in Gold Bars With This Book

Whether you're new to investing or seeking to diversify your portfolio, this beginner-friendly guide will give you the knowledge and confidence to invest in gold, and other precious metals.

https://www.amazon.com/Ultimate-Investing-Buying-Guide-Beginners-ebook/dp/B0F1KWWDXG

# Learn How To Invest in Silver With This Book

Whether you're approaching retirement or already enjoying it, protecting and growing your wealth is critical. The Ultimate Silver Investing & Buying Guide For Beginners is your clear, no-nonsense guide to incorporating silver into your wealth-building strategy.

https://www.amazon.com/Ultimate-Silver-Investing-Buying-Beginners-ebook

# Copyright

Title: Investing In Gold and Silver While Managing Debt
Author: Roggie Clark

# Disclaimer

The views and opinions expressed in this book are those of the author and do not necessarily reflect the official policy or position of any individual, company, or organization cited or referenced in the text. The author is not affiliated with any of the individuals, companies, or organizations mentioned in the text, nor does the author receive any form of compensation for citing or referencing them.

The professional information in this text is distributed on an "as is" basis, without warranty. While every precaution has been taken in the preparation of the text, neither the author nor the publisher shall have any liability to any person or entity with respect to any loss or damage caused or alleged to be caused directly or indirectly by the instructions contained in this text or by the computer software and hardware products described in it.

The author nor the publisher does not guarantee any specific results or outcomes, and the information provided in this text should not be construed as professional advice. Readers should always consult with a qualified professional before making any significant changes to their website or business.

By reading this text, you agree that the author nor the publisher is responsible for any direct, indirect, incidental, or consequential damages that may arise from the use of the information provided. You assume full responsibility for any actions taken based on the information presented in this text.

# Table of Contents

# Introduction

Many people believe they must choose between paying off debt and investing. They are told to eliminate every balance first before even thinking about building assets. Others are told to ignore debt and invest aggressively no matter what. Both extremes create confusion.

The truth is simpler. Investing is always a good idea. The question is not whether you should invest while managing debt. The question is how to do it intelligently.

This book will show you how to think clearly about gold and silver investing while responsibly managing credit cards, student loans, and other financial obligations.

## You Do Not Have To Choose

Debt and investing are not mutually exclusive.

You can aggressively reduce high interest debt while still building small, disciplined positions in precious metals. You can follow a structured repayment plan while protecting yourself against inflation and long term currency risk.

The mistake most people make is adopting an all or nothing mindset. They either invest recklessly while ignoring their debt, or they postpone investing indefinitely out of fear.

Neither approach builds confidence or long term stability.

The goal is balance. You reduce risk while still building assets.

## The Right Way To Think About Debt And Investing

Debt has a cost. That cost is measured in interest rates, cash flow pressure, and psychological stress. Investing has potential return, protection value, and long term compounding benefits.

The key is understanding how these forces interact.

High interest credit card debt demands aggressive attention. Lower interest structured debt, such as certain student loans, may allow room for consistent investing at the same time.

This is not about emotion. It is about structure.

You must understand the math behind interest rates, opportunity cost, and risk before making decisions. When you remove emotion, the strategy becomes clearer.

## How This Book Will Help You

This book will walk you through the decision making process step by step.

You will learn how to evaluate different types of debt, how to rank them by urgency, and how to allocate money between repayment and precious metals exposure. You will understand when to prioritize debt reduction more aggressively and how to build gold and silver positions without creating financial strain.

Most importantly, you will learn how to avoid extremes.

You do not need to eliminate every obligation before investing. You also should not ignore high interest debt in the name of asset building. There is a disciplined middle ground.

## Last Thoughts

Managing debt while investing is not about perfection. It is about control.

When you understand the structure of your debt and the role of gold and silver in your financial plan, you stop reacting emotionally. You start acting intentionally.

In the next chapter, we will begin by examining why investing still matters even when you carry debt, and how proper structure changes the entire conversation.

# Chapter 1: Investing While In Debt Is About Structure

Carrying debt does not cancel your ability to build wealth. What it does require is structure.

Many people approach debt emotionally. They feel guilt, stress, or urgency. At the same time, investing can also trigger emotion, especially when headlines talk about inflation, recession, or financial crisis. When emotion drives decisions, structure disappears.

This chapter is about restoring structure. Investing while managing debt is not reckless. It simply requires clear thinking.

## Why Investing Still Matters

Even if you have debt, time still matters.

Markets do not pause while you pay down balances. Inflation does not wait until you are debt free. Currency purchasing power continues to shift. Gold and silver exist partly to hedge against long term monetary risk.

If you postpone investing for years while focusing only on debt, you may miss valuable time in the market. That does not mean you ignore debt. It means you avoid the assumption that investing must stop completely.

Wealth building and debt reduction can happen simultaneously when handled intelligently.

The goal is not to invest aggressively. The goal is to remain engaged in asset ownership while managing liabilities responsibly.

## The Role Of Precious Metals

Gold and silver serve a specific purpose.

They are not growth stocks. They are not high yield investments. They are monetary metals. They act as insurance against inflation, currency devaluation, and systemic instability.

When you carry debt, especially long term debt, monetary risk still exists. If inflation rises, your purchasing power declines. If currency weakens, your savings lose value.

Small, disciplined positions in gold and silver can serve as financial ballast. They do not eliminate debt, but they can provide psychological and strategic stability.

The key is sizing. Precious metals should not crowd out debt repayment. They should complement it.

## Separating Emotion From Math

Emotion is the enemy of financial progress.

Some people refuse to invest until they feel perfectly secure. Others invest aggressively to compensate for anxiety about debt. Both reactions are emotional.

Instead, focus on math.

What is the interest rate on your credit cards? What is the rate on your student loans? What is your realistic expected return from precious metals over time? What is your cash flow margin?

When you compare these numbers clearly, decisions become less dramatic.

High interest credit card debt demands aggressive repayment. That is math. Lower interest structured loans may allow for steady investing alongside repayment. That is math.

Structure replaces emotion.

## Last Thoughts

Investing while in debt is not about denial. It is about discipline.

You can build assets while reducing liabilities. You can invest responsibly without pretending debt does not exist. The difference lies in structure, not avoidance.

In the next chapter, we will break down the different types of debt and how to rank them properly so your strategy reflects reality instead of fear.

# Chapter 2: Understanding Your Debt Clearly

Before you decide how much to invest and how aggressively to pay down balances, you need clarity. Not all debt is equal. Not all interest rates carry the same urgency. Not all obligations create the same financial pressure.

Too many people lump all debt into one emotional category. That creates confusion and paralysis. Instead, you need to break your debt into clear segments and evaluate each one objectively.

This chapter will help you understand what you are actually dealing with.

## High Interest Credit Cards

High interest credit card debt is the most dangerous type of consumer debt.

Interest rates on credit cards often sit in double digits and can exceed twenty percent. At those levels, compounding works against you aggressively. Every month that balance remains unpaid, it grows quickly.

Mathematically, high interest credit card debt almost always deserves priority. The guaranteed cost of that interest typically outweighs the uncertain return of investing.

That does not mean you stop investing entirely. But it does mean that aggressive repayment should dominate your financial focus.

If you are carrying large credit card balances, your strategy must reflect the urgency of eliminating them.

## Student Loans And Structured Debt

Student loans are different.

Some carry low fixed interest rates. Others may have variable rates or higher costs. Government backed loans often offer structured repayment options, income based plans, or temporary relief programs.

Because of this structure, student loans are not always an emergency in the same way credit cards are.

If your student loan rate is relatively low, and you have stable income, it may be reasonable to invest modestly while paying them down steadily.

The key is understanding the rate and the terms. Fixed low interest debt creates more flexibility than high variable debt.

Clarity replaces fear.

## Personal Loans And Other Obligations

Personal loans, medical debt, and other obligations fall somewhere in the middle.

Some personal loans carry moderate interest rates. Others may approach credit card levels. Medical debt may be interest free in some cases but damaging to credit if ignored.

You must examine each obligation individually.

Ask simple questions. What is the interest rate? Is it fixed or variable? What is the monthly payment? What happens if I delay repayment?

When you separate debt by structure and cost, strategy becomes easier.

### Ranking Debt By Risk

Once you understand the types of debt you carry, the next step is ranking them.

Start with interest rate. Higher rates generally mean higher urgency.

Next, consider stability. Variable rates introduce uncertainty. Fixed rates provide predictability.

Then consider psychological pressure. Some debts cause more stress than others. While math should drive decisions, psychological weight still matters because it affects behavior.

Create a simple ranking system. High interest credit cards at the top. Moderate rate personal loans in the middle. Lower rate structured debt toward the bottom.

When you rank debt clearly, your allocation between repayment and investing becomes structured instead of reactive.

## Last Thoughts

Understanding your debt removes fear from the equation.

High interest credit cards demand urgency. Structured loans allow more flexibility. Personal obligations must be evaluated individually.

Once you know what you are dealing with, you can build a strategy that reflects reality instead of anxiety.

In the next chapter, we will break down the math that drives smart decisions, including how to compare interest rates to expected returns without overcomplicating the process.

# Chapter 3: The Math That Drives Smart Decisions

Emotion creates confusion. Math creates clarity.

When people debate whether to invest or pay off debt, they often argue from extremes. One side says eliminate all debt before investing. The other says invest aggressively and let debt sit. Neither side usually breaks the issue down properly.

The real answer lives in the numbers.

This chapter will help you compare interest rates, expected returns, and risk without overcomplicating the decision.

## Interest Rates vs Expected Returns

Start with a simple comparison.

If you are paying twenty percent interest on a credit card, that is a guaranteed negative return. Eliminating that balance produces a guaranteed twenty percent improvement in your financial position.

Gold and silver do not produce guaranteed returns. They can rise, fall, or move sideways for long periods. Over time, they tend to protect purchasing power, but they are not high yield growth assets.

If your debt carries very high interest, the math clearly favors aggressive repayment.

However, if your debt carries a lower fixed rate, for example four or five percent, the comparison becomes more balanced. In that case, steady investing while paying down debt may make sense.

The key difference is certainty. Debt interest is guaranteed. Investment returns are uncertain.

Structure your decisions around that distinction.

## Opportunity Cost Without Overthinking

Opportunity cost simply means what you give up when choosing one option over another.

If you send every extra dollar to debt and invest nothing, you may miss years of asset accumulation. If you invest aggressively and ignore high interest debt, you may pay thousands in unnecessary interest.

The goal is not to optimize perfectly. The goal is to avoid obvious mistakes.

If high interest debt exists, direct the majority of extra cash there. If lower interest structured debt exists, allow room for disciplined investing.

You do not need complex spreadsheets. You need common sense guided by numbers.

Balance reduces regret.

## Risk Adjusted Thinking

The final piece is risk.

Paying off debt produces a guaranteed return equal to the interest rate. Investing in gold and silver produces uncertain returns with potential upside and downside.

Risk adjusted thinking asks: is the potential return worth the volatility?

With very high interest debt, the answer is usually no. With lower rate debt, the answer may be yes, especially if you value diversification and long term purchasing power protection.

Also consider income stability. If your income is uncertain, reducing debt may provide psychological and financial safety. If your income is stable and predictable, balanced investing may feel more manageable.

Risk is personal, but math provides the foundation.

## Last Thoughts

Smart financial decisions come from comparing certainty against uncertainty.

High interest debt creates guaranteed drag. Gold and silver offer long term protection but no guarantees. When you understand that difference, the decision becomes structured instead of emotional.

You do not have to choose one extreme. You simply allocate intelligently based on the numbers in front of you.

In the next chapter, we will focus specifically on credit card debt and how to build a disciplined strategy while aggressively reducing it.

# Chapter 4: Credit Card Debt Strategy

Credit card debt changes the conversation.

Unlike lower rate structured loans, high interest credit cards create rapid financial drag. They compound against you. They shrink cash flow. They increase stress. If you are serious about building wealth, you cannot ignore this type of debt.

This chapter is about being direct. High interest credit card balances must be handled aggressively. But that does not mean investing disappears entirely.

## Why High Interest Debt Must Be Attacked

Credit card interest rates are often among the highest forms of consumer debt. Double digit rates are common. In some cases, rates exceed twenty percent.

At those levels, repayment becomes a priority.

Every dollar sitting on a high interest card is costing you guaranteed money. There is no market investment that offers a guaranteed return equal to eliminating that balance.

If you carry significant credit card debt, the majority of your extra cash should go toward reducing it. This is not emotional advice. It is mathematical reality.

Aggressive repayment increases cash flow. Increased cash flow increases flexibility. Flexibility creates long term stability.

Eliminating high interest debt is a foundation move.

## Investing While Aggressively Paying It Down

Here is where structure matters.

Aggressive repayment does not require a complete pause in investing. It requires proportion.

You may choose to direct eighty or ninety percent of surplus cash toward debt while allocating a small, consistent amount toward gold and silver. This keeps you engaged in asset ownership without ignoring the urgency of repayment.

Why does this matter?

Because investing builds discipline and momentum. It keeps you focused on long term wealth even while solving short term liabilities.

The key is that investing remains modest and controlled while credit card balances are high.

Debt gets priority. Investing continues in measured form.

## Avoiding All Or Nothing Thinking

All or nothing thinking is dangerous.

Some people decide they will invest nothing until every debt is gone. Others decide debt does not matter and invest aggressively while balances grow.

Both approaches create problems.

If you wait too long to invest, you may delay wealth building unnecessarily. If you invest recklessly while high interest debt compounds, you create financial strain.

Balance is the answer.

High interest debt gets attacked with urgency. Investing continues in a controlled, proportional way. As balances fall, allocation toward investing can increase.

This creates forward movement in both directions.

## Last Thoughts

Credit card debt demands seriousness. It is not neutral. It works against you quickly and consistently.

But investing does not have to stop entirely while you eliminate it.

When you combine aggressive repayment with disciplined, modest investing, you avoid extremes. You reduce liabilities while still building assets.

In the next chapter, we will shift to student loans and other structured debt, where the strategy becomes more flexible and long term in nature.

# Chapter 5: Student Loans And Long Term Debt Strategy

Student loans and other structured debt require a different mindset than credit card balances.

While credit card debt often demands urgent elimination due to high interest rates, many student loans carry fixed, predictable rates and structured repayment terms. This changes the strategy.

The goal here is not panic. It is structure and consistency.

## Fixed vs Variable Rates

The first question to ask about student loans is simple: is the rate fixed or variable?

Fixed rate loans provide stability. You know exactly what you will pay over time. This predictability allows you to plan both repayment and investing without fear of sudden cost increases.

Variable rate loans introduce uncertainty. If rates rise, your monthly payment can increase. This may justify a more aggressive repayment strategy, especially during rising interest rate environments.

If your student loan carries a relatively low fixed rate, for example three to five percent, it may not demand the same urgency as high interest credit card debt.

The structure of the loan determines the strategy.

## Psychological vs Mathematical Payoff

There are two ways to look at debt repayment: mathematically and psychologically.

Mathematically, you should prioritize higher interest rates first. That reduces total interest paid over time.

Psychologically, some people prefer eliminating smaller balances first for motivation. Others prefer clearing a single large obligation to feel progress.

Neither approach is wrong. What matters is consistency.

When it comes to student loans, the math often suggests steady repayment rather than extreme acceleration, especially if rates are moderate. However, if the psychological burden is heavy, accelerating repayment may provide emotional relief.

Financial strategy should not ignore psychology, but it should not be ruled by it either.

Balance both perspectives.

## Investing Consistently During Repayment

Student loans often last many years. Waiting until they are completely eliminated before investing may delay wealth building unnecessarily.

If your rates are moderate and income is stable, consistent investing during repayment can make sense.

You may allocate a defined percentage of income toward repayment and another percentage toward gold and silver exposure. This creates parallel progress.

As your loan balance declines, you can gradually increase your investment allocation.

The key is sustainability. Do not overextend. Do not strain cash flow. Maintain emergency savings while executing your plan.

Consistency over time matters more than short bursts of intensity.

## Last Thoughts

Student loans and other structured debt require patience and perspective.

Fixed, moderate rate debt does not demand panic. It demands structure. You can repay steadily while building assets at the same time.

The strategy shifts from urgency to balance.

In the next chapter, we will bring everything together and outline how to build a balanced plan that prioritizes emergency savings, allocates intelligently between debt and metals, and keeps you financially stable throughout the process.

# Chapter 6: Building A Balanced Plan

Knowledge without structure leads to inconsistency.

You now understand the difference between high interest credit cards and structured loans. You understand how to compare interest rates to expected returns. The next step is building a practical system you can follow every month.

A balanced plan protects you from emergencies, reduces liabilities, and builds assets at the same time.

## Emergency Fund First

Before increasing investing or accelerating debt repayment aggressively, you need a buffer.

An emergency fund protects you from unexpected expenses, job interruptions, medical bills, or urgent repairs. Without it, you may be forced to rely on credit cards again, undoing your progress.

The goal is stability.

A basic emergency fund should cover essential expenses for a defined period. The exact amount depends on your situation, but the principle remains the same. Stability comes first.

Gold and silver are not substitutes for cash reserves. They are long term monetary assets, not short term liquidity tools.

Secure your foundation before increasing allocation elsewhere.

## Allocation Between Debt And Metals

Once your emergency buffer is in place, allocation becomes the focus.

If high interest credit card debt exists, the majority of surplus income should be directed toward repayment. A smaller, disciplined portion can go toward gold and silver.

If debt carries moderate fixed rates, allocation can become more balanced.

The key is intentional percentages. Do not guess month to month. Decide on a structured allocation and follow it consistently.

For example, you may choose to direct a defined portion toward debt and another defined portion toward metals. As balances decline, you gradually shift more toward investing.

Clarity eliminates hesitation.

## Position Sizing While In Debt

Position sizing protects you from overexposure.

While managing debt, gold and silver positions should remain proportional to your financial strength. They should not strain your cash flow or delay necessary repayment.

Small, consistent purchases can be more powerful than irregular large ones. This keeps you disciplined and reduces emotional decision making.

As debt decreases and cash flow improves, your position size can increase naturally.

The process becomes progressive rather than extreme.

## Last Thoughts

A balanced plan is not complicated. It requires three elements: stability, allocation, and discipline.

Build your emergency fund. Attack high interest debt with urgency. Invest consistently and proportionally in gold and silver. Adjust as your financial position improves.

You do not need perfection. You need structure.

In the next chapter, we will focus specifically on how to invest in gold and silver safely while managing debt, including avoiding leverage and emotional buying mistakes.

# Chapter 7: How To Invest In Gold And Silver Safely

When you are managing debt, safety matters even more.

This is not the time for speculation, leverage, or emotional decision making. Gold and silver should serve as stabilizers within your financial plan, not sources of additional risk.

This chapter will focus on practical, conservative approaches to investing in precious metals while you are still reducing liabilities.

## Physical Metals vs ETFs

There are two primary ways beginners gain exposure to gold and silver: physical metals or exchange traded funds.

Physical metals include coins and bars that you purchase and store yourself or through a secure facility. They offer direct ownership. There is no counterparty risk tied to a brokerage or financial institution. Many investors appreciate the tangible nature of physical gold and silver.

ETFs provide exposure to metal prices without physical storage. They are liquid, easy to buy and sell, and convenient within retirement accounts. However, they rely on financial structures and custodians.

While managing debt, simplicity matters. Choose the format you understand and can manage comfortably.

Avoid overcomplicating your strategy. The goal is steady exposure, not complexity.

## Avoiding Leverage

Leverage magnifies outcomes.

Borrowing money to invest in gold or silver while already carrying debt introduces unnecessary risk. If prices decline, losses are amplified. If interest costs exist on borrowed funds, the pressure increases.

While managing debt, leverage works against discipline.

Gold and silver are long term monetary assets, not short term trading vehicles. There is no need to amplify exposure with margin accounts, futures contracts, or borrowed capital.

Stay unleveraged. Keep positions fully paid for. Protect your cash flow.

Stability always comes before acceleration.

## Avoiding Emotional Purchases

Precious metals often attract emotion.

Headlines about inflation, banking instability, or geopolitical tension can create urgency. Social media can amplify fear. Market rallies can create excitement.

While managing debt, emotional buying is dangerous.

Stick to a plan. Purchase at predetermined intervals or allocation percentages. Avoid reacting to short term price spikes or panic driven narratives.

Discipline matters more than timing.

Consistent, measured purchases reduce stress and keep your strategy aligned with your overall financial structure.

## Last Thoughts

Gold and silver can serve a valuable role in your financial plan, but only when approached responsibly.

Choose a format you understand. Avoid leverage. Avoid emotional decision making. Keep positions proportional while debt remains.

Safety and structure are your priorities.

In the final chapter, we will focus on long term discipline and how to adjust your allocation as debt decreases and your financial position strengthens.

# Chapter 8: Long Term Discipline And Adjustments

Debt reduction and investing are not static processes. They evolve.

As balances decline and cash flow improves, your strategy should adjust. What begins as a heavily debt focused plan can gradually transition into a more investment centered structure. The key is not sudden change, but steady progression.

This chapter focuses on discipline over time.

## Increasing Allocation As Debt Falls

When high interest debt decreases, you free up cash flow. That creates opportunity.

Instead of allowing lifestyle inflation to consume the difference, redirect that freed cash intentionally. A portion can increase your gold and silver allocation. Another portion may strengthen other investments or retirement accounts.

The shift should be gradual and structured.

As debt declines:

- Investment percentages can increase.
- Emergency reserves can be strengthened.
- Financial flexibility expands.

Your allocation evolves with your financial health.

The important point is progression, not perfection.

## Staying Consistent During Stress

Financial stress does not disappear overnight.

Markets fluctuate. Metal prices rise and fall. Economic headlines create anxiety. Unexpected expenses may still appear.

Consistency protects you.

If you have built an emergency fund, structured your repayment, and defined your investment allocation, you reduce the temptation to react impulsively.

When gold or silver prices drop, discipline prevents panic selling. When prices surge, discipline prevents reckless overbuying.

Stress tests your plan. Structure protects it.

## Avoiding Fear And Hype

Gold and silver attract strong narratives.

During economic uncertainty, fear based messaging increases. During price rallies, hype spreads quickly. Both extremes can distort rational thinking.

While managing debt, fear and hype are especially dangerous. They can push you to overallocate to metals out of anxiety or abandon your strategy entirely out of frustration.

Stay anchored to fundamentals.

Gold and silver serve as monetary protection and diversification tools. They are not lottery tickets. They are not emergency substitutes for cash.

Ignore dramatic predictions. Follow your structured allocation.

## Last Thoughts

Long term wealth building requires adjustment, not reaction.

As debt decreases, your flexibility increases. As flexibility increases, your investing capacity expands. The transition should be intentional and steady.

You are not choosing between debt responsibility and investing. You are integrating both into a disciplined system.

In the final section, we will summarize the key takeaways and provide a clear framework you can follow moving forward.

# Conclusion

Managing debt while investing in gold and silver is not about choosing sides. It is about structure.

Throughout this book, you have seen that investing does not need to stop just because debt exists. At the same time, debt cannot be ignored in the name of wealth building. Both realities can exist together when handled intelligently.

Now let us simplify everything.

## Key Takeaways In Plain English

High interest credit card debt demands urgency. It creates guaranteed financial drag and should be attacked aggressively.

Lower rate structured debt, such as many student loans, allows more flexibility. It can often be repaid steadily while investing continues in parallel.

Gold and silver are not growth assets. They are monetary protection tools. They should be sized proportionally, especially while debt remains.

Emergency savings come first. Stability supports both repayment and investing.

Structure eliminates emotional extremes.

When you understand these core principles, the tension between debt and investing becomes manageable.

## A Clear Framework You Can Follow

First, build an emergency fund.

Second, rank your debt by interest rate and risk.

Third, direct the majority of extra cash toward high interest balances while maintaining modest, disciplined precious metals exposure.

Fourth, as high interest debt declines, gradually increase your investment allocation.

Fifth, remain consistent. Avoid reacting to headlines or short term price movements.

This framework removes confusion. It replaces fear with process.

### Final Thoughts On Wealth And Responsibility

Wealth building and responsibility are not opposites.

Paying down debt is responsible. Building assets is responsible. Protecting purchasing power is responsible.

The mistake is believing you must perfect one before beginning the other.

Financial progress is layered. You stabilize. You reduce liabilities. You build assets. You adjust as your position improves.

Discipline matters more than speed. Structure matters more than intensity.

## Last Thoughts

You do not need to eliminate every obligation before investing. You do not need to invest aggressively while ignoring high interest debt.

You need balance.

When you approach gold and silver investing with discipline, clarity, and proportion, you build strength instead of stress.

Now you have a framework. The next step is implementation.

# About the Author

Roggie "Raj" Clark is an entrepreneur, author, and education minded creator whose work spans digital marketing, investing, economics, programming, and early academic development. With more than a decade of experience in ecommerce and digital business growth, he has built and managed successful online stores with thousands of sales and consulted for numerous marketing clients on branding, consumer behavior, and online strategy.

As a former marketing manager at a fintech company, Roggie gained firsthand experience in financial systems, wealth building strategy, and economic decision making. That experience inspired him to write books focused on investing, financial literacy, macro and microeconomics, and helping readers make informed long term financial decisions.

Roggie also holds a degree in Elementary Education and has a background in classroom teaching. Drawing from his academic training and educational experience, he has written classroom aligned books designed to support learning standards and structured skill development. His educational titles are intentionally crafted to blend clear instruction with engaging content that supports both classroom and homeschool learning environments.

Whether explaining search engine optimization, programming concepts such as HTML, CSS, and JavaScript, economic principles, or foundational academic skills, Roggie focuses on breaking complex topics into accessible learning experiences. Across every subject he writes about, his goal is to build strong foundations, encourage critical thinking, and equip readers with tools that support long term growth.

He lives in Maryland and continues to develop educational and business focused resources designed to inform, empower, and inspire.

www.ingramcontent.com/pod-product-compliance
Lightning Source LLC
LaVergne TN
LVHW022324200926
848481LV00004B/1427

* 9 7 9 8 2 9 5 6 7 2 5 0 7 *